The Wing Walker

The Life and Times
Of
Irene Maude O'Connor Carlberg

Bernard J. Fleury, Ed.D.

Printed by Create Space, an Amazon.com Company.

ISBN-13: 978-1544814810

ISBN-10: 154481481X

Website: www.intolifebylight.com

Printed in the United States of America

DEDICATION

To my sister Judy Johnson, Mother Irene's loving and faithful daughter. It has been my privilege to be your adopted brother from the day Mother adopted me.

TABLE OF CONTENTS

REVIEWS

The Wing Walker: The Life and Times of Irene Maude O'Connor Carlberg is a nonfiction biography written by Bernard J. Fleury, Ed.D. Irene was born in 1909 to Rose and Patrick O'Connor. Patrick wasn't her mom's first husband; she had been married before that to an older, well-to-do, handicapped man at her parents' urging. Rose was young, wild and impulsive, however, and her adventure climbing up Mt. Monadnock in the company of two male hikers caused her first husband to divorce her. Irene took after her mom in her enthusiasm for excitement and adventure, and her dad fully supported her and her siblings. In her teens, Irene discovered motorcycles and airplanes and surprised her male friends by her willingness to be a daredevil, including her stunt of walking out on a wing of her friend's plane. While her first marriage, when she was still a teen, was not a success, her second one to Sailor Carlberg was a match made for life. Irene was an accomplished seamstress and artist, specializing in oil painting, and had a number of showings of her artwork. When she was in her 90's, she asked her friend, who was the Deacon at the Catholic Church she attended, if he would agree to her adopting him. She had always wanted a son, and the author, who was 67 years old at the time, was thrilled and proud to agree.

The Wing Walker is one of those biographies that you really don't want to miss out on. Fleury is a naturally gifted storyteller, and his affection for, and admiration of, his second mother shines out on every page of this remarkable work. Reading about Irene and her mother's exploits at times in the past when women's roles were strictly circumscribed is refreshing and inspirational. I was especially interested in those parts of the biography that detailed Irene's experiences caring for the disabled at the State Hospital and the descriptions of her artwork and creative process. Fleury also includes his autobiography in this work, and it ties in so well with his second mother's life story. I loved studying the photographs he included and found the time spent engrossed in his stories to be well-spent and utterly enjoyable. The Wing Walker is most highly recommended.

Reviewer: Jack Magnus, Readers' Favorite, Rating *****

The Wing Walker: The Life and Times of Irene Maude O'Connor Carlberg by Bernard J Fleury is the fascinating biography of a woman who made a difference in a male-dominated world, born at a time when the headlines were filled with stories of adventure and strong beginnings — William Howard Taft in the first year of his presidency, the NAACP getting organized in New York and headed by W.E.B. DuBois, the planting of the United States flag at the North Pole by Robert E. Peary, and a lot more. It is against the backdrop of a surprising evolving history that Carlberg's personality emerges. Born in 1909, she lived up to ninety-nine years, a costume maker and a nationally recognized folk artist. Exceptional and bold in character, she set out to make a difference in a male-dominated culture. It was this boldness of hers that moved her to stand on the wings of a biplane in flight, sail down the frozen Connecticut River holding a sheet, ride in the basket of a hot air balloon at 98, and do a lot of other fascinating things.

The Wing Walker is told in the voice of Irene Maude O'Connor Carlberg, clear and compelling, and it is interesting to notice the historical details in the narrative. The biography allows readers a wonderful understanding of American culture in the twentieth century and demonstrates the evolution through the twenty-first century. Readers encounter the empowering figure of a woman who fought for equality, an inspiring story reflecting the ideals of the feminist movements that have shaped history. The Wing Walker is told in a light and engaging tone and is filled with humor. It is, indeed, a refreshing read.

Reviewer: Ruffina Oserio, Readers' Favorite, Rating *****

The Wing Walker by Bernard J Fleury tells The Life and Times Of Irene Maude O'Connor Carlberg. Irene was one of the great feminists, a woman who really pushed the boundaries of what women could do. Nothing could tame her adventurous spirit, such as motorcycle riding as a teenager, driving all over the place and even driving a stock car. Irene was the woman on the biplane wings when it flew. She was the woman who took off down the Connecticut River while it was frozen, with just a sheet for a sail. Costume designer extraordinaire, getting her motorcycle license in her 60's, riding in hot air balloons in her 90s; join Irene as she takes us through her entire life in one joyful, exhilarating story.

The Wing Walker: The Life and Times of Irene Maude O'Connor Carlberg by Bernard J Fleury is an amazing story, albeit a short one. She really was a wonderful, spirited woman and Bernard tells her story so well. She had a life of adventure, living it for herself and living for each day. Nothing stood in her way of doing what she wanted, rather than what was expected of her and Bernard writes her story in a real way; no fluff, just straightforward words, her words. The addition of the photographs was a nice touch, bringing the story even more to life and allowing us a real glimpse into her life, not just through words. This isn't a chronological book; it weaves back and forth through her life, highlighting everything this wonderful woman achieved. It's a real eyeopener; if you enjoy true stories then you will love The Wing Walker.

    Reviewer: Anne-Marie Reynolds, Readers' Favorite, Rating *****

Bernard J. Fleury, Ed.D.

THE WINGWALKER

The Life and Times
Of
Irene Maude O'Connor Carlberg

INTRODUCTION

America has been blessed with many bold, daring, ahead-of-their-time women. Irene Carlberg is one of those women who lived ninety-one years in the 20th Century and eight years, two months in the 21st Century. When she saw a biplane, she wanted to ride on its wings—a motorcycle, she had to drive it—another plane, she had to fly it. A costume maker, a nationally recognized folk artist, a coach to children learning to dance and their taxi driver everywhere—mentally ill persons in a large impersonal hospital, she served them in every way she could including advocating for them to her own detriment! But like the rest of people, especially when we were young, we make mistakes, sometimes nearly fatal ones! Her first short marriage at the early age of seventeen, and its violent end, could have ruined the rest of her life. She defended herself in the best way she could in the legal atmosphere of the early 20th Century wherein women were at a definite disadvantage when it came to divorce and child support. She fought to survive poor decisions on her part, for herself and her child's sake, and as we'll read in her story, she went on to live a creative life of hard work, and loving giving, to her family and many others as well.

This is her story told in her own words as she wrote or spoke them to her "adopted" son.

Special thanks to mother Irene's daughters Sonja and Judith who accepted me into their family. A person, who is gifted with one wonderful mother as I was, is fortunate indeed. I am the most fortunate of men since 1999 when Irene Carlberg who had three daughters, one of whom, Rose, is deceased, told me she always wanted a son also, and asked me if I would be her son! Sonja and Judy welcomed me, so I said "yes" and at the age of sixty-seven got a second wonderful mother!

Now, for her story.

CHAPTER ONE: IT ALL BEGINS

I was born in Cooley Dickinson Hospital on May 5th 1909 to Rose Putnam Chickering O'Connor and Patrick Joseph O'Connor. That was the year when in Sports, the Pittsburgh Pirates won the World Series beating the Detroit Tigers, 4 – 3, Belgian bicyclist Francois Faber won the Tour de France, and Arthur Gore and Penelope Boothby both won Wimbledon singles.

What it cost to live was reflected in the price of foodstuffs. Butter was thirty-five cents a pound. A ten-pound bag of potatoes sold for nineteen cents and five pounds of flour for eighteen cents. Corn was the most valuable product in America.

The Headlines were filled with stories of adventure and new beginnings:

William Howard Taft was in the first year of his presidency.

The NAACP was organized in New York and headed by W.E.B. DuBois.

Commander Robert E. Peary planted the United States Flag at the North Pole.

Henry Ford began assembly-line-production of motorcars. Eventually, he produced 19,051 Model T cars and led the auto industry because of their popularity.

Bakelite was developed and became the first commercially marketed plastic.

Helen Hayes, at age 9, opened in <u>Old Dutch</u>, her first New York appearance.

The first notable animated motion picture was <u>Gertie the Dinosaur</u>.

The first permanent waves were given by London hairdressers, and Guglielmo Marconi won the Nobel Prize for Physics and radio shows and news were our main means of entertainment. Of course, I was unaware of any of this at the time being immersed in keeping Ma and Pa busy caring for me.

Ma and Pa

My mother told me that when she was a teenager she was rambunctious and in those days that meant she wasn't too obedient and as a girl you were always supposed to be good and mind your folks. They (her folks) decided she should marry a well-to-do man who was a bow-legged cripple and had a cottage at the foot of Bald Hill in Milford, New Hampshire. The man was named Jesse Chickering and the little rustic cottage had a pond in the back yard that was just filled with beautiful white pond lilies. When you went out in a rowboat you would pull up huge bunches of them and they smelt so sweet and clean!

Now, I'll ramble on a bit. Ma was young. Uncle Jesse, as I came to call him, was old and crippled. My mom was full of piss and vinegar and kicked up the traces once in awhile. She was the first female to climb the sheer side of Mt. Monadnock, which she did in bloomers (horrors). In those days ladies didn't show their ankles, as that was a sign that you were the Devils Disciple. Also she had two male companions along with her on her climb. Well it was cause for divorce, which was also a desperate measure to take in those days. Jessie divorced her in a hurry. Now I really have managed to get ahead of my story. Before this dreadful episode Ma had a son. He was a huge baby. He weighed ten or eleven pounds and mother told me the walls, and even part of the low ceiling, was covered with blood spots in the birthing process. She was vague on the happenings from then on but, she said the next thing she knew she was in a box or something on the table and the room was filled with weeping friends and relatives. It became apparent she was being waked. She kept moving her hand and finally someone realized she was alive and took her out of the casket and put her into bed. Mother said it was the very worst thing she ever went through. In those days they didn't embalm so that would surely have been the worst way to die. Imagine being buried alive, but that happened quite often in those olden days. Well, she recovered and took baby George and went back home to live on the farm with her parents, who felt disgraced. Jesse was getting lonesome and asked her to come back and live with him once more. Ma said "no way" although she did go down to the cottage to clean and cook for him about once a week. Mother stayed on with her parents and became an expert seamstress learning both to sew and draft patterns. Her trade was called Garment Making. She did a lot of traveling teaching the trade to other ladies. Finally her lectures landed her in Northampton where she some how met my father-to-be, who was widowed and raising three daughters, "Mary, Bessie, and Helen". She was Protestant and Dad was Catholic. They were married by a minister. Pa's name was Patrick Joseph O'Connor and he had come over from County Cork in the Old Sod and I always thought he still had a bit of old Ireland in his system, as he sure had some fantastic stories to tell. He'd tell about spooks rising out of the graveyard at night when he was on his way home. He said many times he'd get to his thatched-roof home, rush in and fall on the kitchen floor. His mother would laugh and tell him that it was only his own shadow behind him when the moon was out. When the wind blew around the corners of our house in the wintertime he'd say the banshee was howling outside and it would get me if I went out at night. In the spring he would tell me that the circle of grass on our front lawn, which was a mossy patch of lighter green than the rest of the lawn, was where the wee-folk lived and had their little dances and if you listened hard you could hear their fiddles playing. If you were real lucky you could see the wee ones dancing up a storm.

Needless to say I spent a great deal of time on the front lawn and never walked on that circle of soft grass. The neighbors used to say, "That O'Connor kid must be a bit daft as she is always crawling around on the front lawn with her ear to the ground."

For years we went to our summer cottage at the foot of Bald Hill in Milford, New Hampshire that Uncle Jesse had left to my mother. My aunts and uncles lived up there and mother used to take me out of school a week early so dad could go too as that was his vacation week. I loved it there! The chickens came right into the kitchen and the horse stuck his head through the open window.

My Pa worked for the State building roads for many years and my Ma continued with her seamstress work though she did most of it at home.

I can remember my mother having the most gorgeous dresses, as she was a wonderful seamstress she made them herself. I especially still remember one dress with "leg-o-mutton" sleeves. It was a most beautiful silk with green, blue, and purple mixed material, and it rustled when she walked.

My father had very little education but he was a very smart man and had an unbelievable memory. When I was growing up he built roads and had many men working under him. He worked for the Massachusetts State Highway department and built the first road over Jacob's Ladder. His territory went from Jacob's Pillow to the Boston Road. He never wrote anything down but could remember the men's names, how many hours they worked, the trucks that were used and how many hours each truck was used. I helped him with the payrolls on Thursday nights and we never had any complaints when the checks were passed out. Many of the men in the crews were Portuguese or Italian and a few of them knew very little English.

The Growing Up Years

We lived in Northampton in a big house on Grant Avenue. I went to Bridge Street School and then to Smith Vocational where I took up cooking and housekeeping. I think it's now called Home Economics.

On Bridge Street there were no sidewalks in those days, just a sandy walk in front of the Rose Tree Inn (now Duffy's Tire). This was a hangout for Smith College girls where they could enjoy a glass of wine and a cigarette. The Madam who owned the Inn was an odd-ball, she dressed in men's clothes most of the time and kept the window shades pulled down so no one could sneak up and peek in. We kids loved her as she would invite us in and she made us mugs of hot chocolate with marshmallows in it. In winter the fireplace had a roaring fire going and we would sit and get warm before going out to ski or slide. We did quite a lot of cross-country skiing (if you could call it that)! It was fun skiing down through the meadows. We would go as far as the bend on the Connecticut River and stop and look at the big white house (better known as the Summit House) on the very top of Mt. Holyoke. The Cable car path could be seen clearly through the pine trees lining it's path. We did a lot of skating on the Connecticut River. The river ice was very thick as the winters were extremely cold. Sometimes we tied a sheet on a pole and used that for a sail. We would fly over the ice and be at Smith's Ferry in no time. Coming back dragging our homemade sails be hind us was torture. We cried frozen tears while fighting the wind and trying to stay upright on our skates. The Hadley Bridge was a welcome sight you can bet. The winters were severe and often freezing rain would make a thick crust on top of the snow. It was usually strong enough to stand on. Once in a while it would break through while we were trying to skate on it and we would get a cut or two, but it was fun anyway. The favorite sliding place of all was Hospital Hill. There was a ski jump there that someone had built. Not too high, but high enough to get a little thrill when you went over it. Another dare from my gang (such good buddies) was I went down the hill and over the jump on a toboggan lying on my belly. Boy did that rattle my bones!! (Didn't do the toboggan any good either) That was the first and last time I did that stupid trick believe me!

Well, time went on and I started to grow up. I liked basketball and all the sports the boys liked. Met a gang of motorcycle guys and gals and got hooked on bikes and planes. I met a barnstormer who had landed his plane down in the meadows. I hung around admiring his plane until he must have thought I was never going to leave. He took pity on me and said he was going up to do a few tricks and would take me up and make me holler "uncle". Little did he know I just never refused a DARE. We did the loop-de-loop and many kinds of scary things and finally a Falling Leaf. We came so close to the ground I was sure we were going to hit either a tree or the ground. It was a real thrill, but I didn't yell "uncle". I couldn't have said "amen" let alone "uncle", but I begged to go up again. The pilot went on his way and I then went down to Atwood Airport where I met a young man whose last name was Lyman and he owned a plane. He was in the Navy and looked real sharp in his uniform. His folks were well to do and they lived on the Lyman Estate off South Street. This was the home where Calvin Coolidge and his better half lived later on. Lyman said I could go up with him if I would go out on the wing. Another Dare? Of course I said okay and up we went. I kept studying how far apart the struts were and when he raised his hand I climbed out, hung onto the struts and got to the end of the wing. Lyman was having a hard time keeping the wing straight as my weight made the plane dip on the side I was on. What a dope I was. I didn't realize I was wearing what was called a butterfly skirt all pleats and very, very wide. I was out on the edge and couldn't see as the skirt was blowing like crazy and up over my head. What to do? I just had to see to get back in the seat. I finally had a brainstorm, fumbled at my girdle, found a safety pin, (bless that guy who invented the safety pin) and I pinned the bottom of my skirt together and crawled back into my seat. Lyman was laughing himself silly. When I managed to pull myself together I looked down, traffic was stopped, everyone was looking up clapping or laughing. No wonder the car horns were blowing! I had dressed in such a hurry that morning that I knew I had my girdle on, but where were my panties? It's a good thing we didn't have cam-recorders in those days! I looked at the paper the next day. Thank goodness there was no mention of anything in the news!

We landed, I stayed in the hanger, then said to hell with it! Some of the bike gang were hanging around watching the fun. We took off in a cloud of dust. The next time I went up with Lyman was the very last time. Geese were flying south minding their own business and Lyman flew right at the leader. I helped him clean the front of the plane and the propeller, said, "So long jackass", and that was that. I read in the paper that he lost his flying license and also got some kind of demotion from the Navy, as they didn't think much of his stupid stunt. No more Atwoods, down to LaFleurs in the Meadows. I made up my mind I was going to do a parachute jump. Posters were around announcing the jump. I was still under age so I had to get both parents okay. Ma was a good skate and she signed but father was something else! He wouldn't sign and went to the airport and got his Irish up. So, no jump for me! I guess Pa's little people must have told him a secret as the man who was going to let me use his chute jumped in Pittsfield and the chute never opened. He always packed his own chute but something must have gone wrong. You can just believe that my father didn't let me forget that episode in a hurry.

I still loved planes, so I hung around Atwoods down on Route 5 every chance I got. Roger Atwood gave me a ride because I teased him so much. He asked if I would like to learn to fly. I told him I didn't have any money but he said, "I'll give you one or two lessons for nothing and then I'll see if I can get your old man to give me some money."

It was wonderful! The plane had a stick to steer it by and Roger told me to watch the Mountain so I knew I was upright and level. I learned to fly, but I never learned how to land.

The Wing Walker

There were a lot of electrical and telephone wires over parts of Atwoods and I was afraid of running into them.

CHAPTER TWO: LLOYD

I graduated from Smith Vocational in June of 1926 at the age of seventeen. During our August 1926 summer vacation at Bald Hill, I met a good-looking, nineteen year old, black-haired guy from Milford, Lloyd Morton Webster. He was a full-blooded Pennacook Indian. We dated a couple of times and on September 20, 1926, knowing I was pregnant, Lloyd came to Northampton, and we were married that day. Since he was a senior in high school, he returned to Milford the next day and I stayed with my folks in Northampton. Lloyd came back to Hamp for a visit on October 14, and the rest of the time I wrote letters to him until February 1927. However, it was pretty clear by the end of December 1926 that Lloyd would not support me and that we would not end up living together. His parents were very unhappy when they found out that we had married. Our baby, Rose, was born premature and had pixie shaped ears and an oval shaped head. It was pointed in the front and back so I had to lay her head sideways on the pillow. She also had a thin, white transparent skin like a mask over her head when she arrived, and a lot of black hair. She was so small I made a bonnet out of a lady's handkerchief. I couldn't buy a bonnet to fit anyway because of the way her head was shaped. In no time her head straightened out and she was a beautiful little girl.

Lloyd graduated from high school in June of 1927 and was supporting his parents and seven brothers and sisters but not me or Rose. My parents and I went to Milford to a Judge Prescott's office where we met with Lloyd and his mother. She told the Judge she didn't want her son to live with me. We had been together less than a year and had never really lived together except for a few days. When he continued to refuse to give any kind of support except for one dollar, I sued for divorce. By this time my dander was up!

My Aunt Mary lived in New Hampshire and was a neighbor and good friend of the Webster Clan. When I took him to court on December 22, 1927, she was there with Lloyd, his mother, Judge Prescott, and Jessie A.G. Andre` of Northampton who were his two lawyers. Funny how supposedly a poor guy from a poor family could afford <u>two lawyers</u>.

I went into court that day with a gun in my pocket. I had found it in a trunk that my half-brother had when he was in the Army. It had been around quite a while and had a sort of greenish stuff on it. My mother, dad and Baby Rose went to court with me. The Judge decided in his favor. So, we left and headed for home. Just as we got to Bridge Street we saw their New Hampshire car parked near the corner where Budgar's Drug Store used to stand. There they were, my Aunt Mary in the front seat, mother-in-law beside Lloyd in the back. I parked my car in back of theirs and got out telling Ma I would only be a minute. When they saw me coming they tried to lock the car doors and wouldn't talk to me. Lloyd got his door locked but the Aunt and mother-in-law weren't quick enough. I got a bit riled up and yanked open the front door and grabbed Aunt Mary and threw her out of the car and onto the sidewalk. Then it was my screeching mother-in-law's turn and out she went too onto the sidewalk. Of course I still had the gun in my pocket. I climbed into the car and bent over toward the back seat where Lloyd was sitting and asked him if he couldn't break down and help me out a little money wise. He said, "No way", so I pulled out the gun and told him I thought he needed another hole in his face! I'm not really sure just what I intended to do, but he looked so scared I started laughing. We struggled, me trying to hold onto the gun and he trying to grab it. A small crowd gathered and a policeman reached in the car and took the gun away from us. I now had no weapon so I started kicking him with my spike heels. Got out of the car and back to my own car and headed for the Hadley Bridge where I threw the holster and extra bullets in the river. We then got Attorney James Henry to represent me and went to the Police Station where I was arrested, taken to court and arraigned and let go on bail posted by Ma. Lloyd, Judge Prescott, and Lloyd's mother were also there. Of course I had to go to court twice on February 28 and 29, 1928. I said that there was a gun and that we fought over it, but it was Lloyd's gun and as both our prints were on it and my dad said that he had seen the gun in Webster's suitcase, I was finally found innocent on March 1, 1928 by the jury, and it was over! The newspaper accounts at the time said that the courtroom was full both times. That was true, but most of the onlookers were my biker friends and school buddies supporting me.

I had a girl friend in Newark, New Jersey who heard about the mess and invited me down there for a visit. My mother said, "Go down there for a little while and things will quiet down around here." I took a bus and away I went.

My friend had a lot of friends, but they were all guys who belonged to the Mafia! This particular group had their headquarters at a taxi company that they owned and used as a cover up while they went about their business. They mostly dealt with spraying acid at cleaning establishments and garment stores, etc. who wouldn't pay protection money. Occasionally something much worse would be discussed!

Their home life was something else. Family meant everything they and their wives were treated with respect. Getting together at night for a Tomato Pie (pizza now) and wine was almost a ritual. I got along fine with most all of them and especially with Aunts and Grandmas although many didn't speak English and I sure didn't speak or understand much Italian. Anyway it was sure a big change from the mostly quiet place of Northampton, Massachusetts. Enough about this time in my life! I was soon home again and very glad to be back.

CHAPTER THREE: "SAILOR" – PARTNER FOR LIFE

Finally there was a bit of local excitement! A Wild West Show at the Fairgrounds, and down I went to see the sights. They had a little bit of everything, bronco riding, calf roping, you name it! The show was called King Brothers Rodeo. I was invited to have breakfast at their cookhouse and went horseback riding down through the meadows. The horse stopped to graze a bit. I gave him a pat under his mane and he dropped down and played dead! Was I scared! Of course I had no idea that the horse was trained to play dead when given the signal of a pat under his mane. He was also the Pony Express Horse in the show.

But, it wasn't all rodeo doings. One thing they had was a motor drome, a very large wooden affair. Outside on a platform were two motorcycles which guys would jump on and rev up, making a lot of noise. One tall blonde with curly hair caught my eye. He rode his bike inside the drome. Noisy it sure was! The other show people told me that he once rode with a lion on the seat behind him and they fell or slid to the floor. Neither one got hurt and the lion kept shaking his head.

All the cowboys and gals had bright colored satin outfits. Well, the show finished and moved on to another town, but by that time the tall blonde and I were a twosome and he stayed in Northampton. He was a blonde handsome Swede with tattoos everywhere!

My father wanted me to stay single and he promised me everything including a car and an airplane. But after a one year courtship Irving, who was nicknamed "Sailor"(because he always wore a seaman's cap) and I were married on May 18, 1932. My "Sailor" was from Maine where he was a Rodeo Rider also and had broken almost every bone in his body at one time or another. After we married, he gave up rodeo entirely and went to work for my dad building roads. I must have a thing for Indian men because Sailor Carlberg also had Indian blood as his mother was Bertha Mountain and she belonged to a branch of the Abnaki Tribe and his father was Swedish. I think "Sokoho" was the small tribe's name. They came from Moosehead Lake district in Maine. But Sailor had blonde hair not black. With both parents dead, he had left home at sixteen, and headed for Boston where he joined the rodeo.

We went to live with my folks in the big house on Grant Avenue along with my daughter Rose. When Rose was ten years old I had a little blonde daughter who looked just like her dad, Sailor. We named her Sonja. A little over two years later I had another little blondie who we named Judith, and that was it!

We now had three girls in all. I bet their dad must have wished for a son at times as we females were a lot to cope with. So with no sons, Judy became his tomboy and his constant companion whether it was cleaning out the chicken coop or whatever.

Both of my parents died in 1936, my Ma in August with cancer and my Pa in October. We continued to live on Grant Avenue and in 1937, the year Sonja was born, the Rodeo came back to Northampton and most of the gang stayed with us when the show was over. They usually went back to Texas but that year we had a house full of guests for most of the winter. My sewing machine worked overtime as I made the girls new satin outfits for their Spring 1938 opening. For years after that we would have <u>one</u> or <u>two</u> of the guys come to see how we were doing and sometimes stay a little while.

Soon after our youngest daughter Judith was born in 1940, the cost of maintaining the large house on Grant Avenue became too much for us so we moved to a smaller house on Woodmont Road and it was there that our daughters grew to maturity and where I still live.

The Adventures of Growing Up With Ma

We went roller-skating even when the weather was too stormy for traveling. One time on our way home from skating, we passed the State Highway plow. (Sailor, my husband worked for the State Highway Dept.). Anyway, the storm was so bad you couldn't see anything at all. We managed to get home, get the car into the garage and jump into our beds, clothes and all. But Dad was too smart for us. He came storming into the house and pulled the blankets off the beds and the jig was up!

He said that he felt the hood of the car and it was still hot. We, and especially me, then got a real lecture. He said, "Next time the State Police say to stay off the roads you stay home! Are you listening?"

He was usually a quiet man but that night I found out he could be loud when he got angry! We were "good" for a while, but not for long!

One foggy night when the girls had skating lessons, we were running late. So we piled in the car and headed for the skating rink in a hurry passing cars along the way. A trooper came along side me and yelled, "Pull Over!" Judy piped up, "Ma, I told you not to go so fast!" The trooper came up to our car and said, "I counted five cars you passed in this heavy fog." Then he took out his pad and started writing.

I quickly got a brainstorm and in my best polite voice I murmured, "My husband drives the big State truck and he plows your barracks out to save you guys a lot of shoveling. I guess I'll have to tell him about this as he isn't supposed to plow you guys out anyway!" He tore up the page and turned around heading for the cruiser. Just before getting in, he turned to me and said, "Don't let me catch you again". But the adventures continued.

One Friday night while at the Roller Rink we decided to go watch the stock car races that were at the old Rhythm Inn Race Track near Lake Wyola in Shutesbury. We piled into our cars and off we went. I got a chance to drive but the car they got for me didn't have any brakes, any doors that would open and no rear window. I got pushed into the car through the back window and the next day I had black and blue hips!

The announcer yelled, "Ma Carlberg, does Pa Carlberg know what you're doing tonight?" Pa Carlberg did as he heard it on the radio!

The flag dropped and away we went! It was a dirt track and at every corner great clouds of dust blanketed the stands and the people near the fence. I didn't win but it was a thrill and I was the last one on the track as I had no brakes. I finally ran into a big bale of hay and that stopped my stock car or else I would have been going until it ran out of gas.

Going to the stock car races wasn't a one-time event! My girls used to come dashing into Pro Brush, where I was working at the time, saying, "Come on Ma, it's time to go to the stock car races!" My boss was Fred Corbertt and he always used to say, "Go on, but if you don't win this one it will be the last time I let you out of work early." He was a good sport!

On another night while I was working at Pro Brush, Sonja and Judy came dashing in (they never just walked). They were all excited and asked if I had seen them on TV. Crazy kids, how could I see them on TV when I was working? Anyway it was the last of February or the first of March, I forget the exact date, and they had had their pictures taken for the Gazette with bathing suits on and they were dancing on the blocks of ice up near the Coolidge Bridge and throwing snowballs at each other! Guess they must have had a little bit of their mother in them, don't you think?

Dancing Girls

Both my daughter Judith and her daughter Judette were dancers.

Judith (Judy) took lessons in tap, ballet and ballroom dancing from Matt and Isabelle Mooney. She started about the age of ten and danced every year at all the recitals. She later took lessons from Elsie Cappel in Holyoke until she graduated from High School.

In later years, her daughter and my grand-daughter, Judette, began at age four, to take dance lessons which included Ballet, Tap, Lyrical and Contortionist Acrobatics from Carol Butlers and later moved on to take lessons from the famous dance master Frank Hatchett who taught at the Dunbar Community Center in Springfield. Judette became a member of the Hatchett Dance Company, which was quite an honor. Frank's dancers performed locally, as well as at the Naval Academy in Maryland, for a Bill Cosby show, as well as in New York. We, her mother and I were always included.

After 18 or so years, Frank moved to New York where he opened a Dance Studio called "The Broadway Dance Center" He became very popular and in demand, and taught such famous people as Madonna, Olivia Newton John, Janet Jackson and Paula Abdul jus to mention a few.

I made all of both Judy's and Judette's costumes until Judette finished dancing, when she married at age twenty-five.

CHAPTER FOUR: MOTHER'S WORK HISTORY

During the war years I worked at American Thread Company in Holyoke making spools of various types of thread. After that during the year the war ended I worked at General Electric in Holyoke putting raw material into pre-forms for a type of cabinet that was used in airplanes. For a short time after that I worked at Twin Cleaners in Northampton. In 1950 I moved on to Pro Brush in Florence where I made dishes, parts for inside washing machines, and a hard rubber part for planes in Alaska so they wouldn't freeze up. Rose grew up and married during those years, Sonja graduated from high school, and Judy was half way through her senior year when I went to work at the State Hospital in Northampton in 1958. For thirteen years until 1971 I worked at that hospital. I was trained to be a charge attendant at the hospital where I worked directly with mentally disabled patients. Being a Charge Nurse, as we were referred to, meant we were responsible for setting up and giving patients their medications. We also did all the housekeeping on the wards, and personal care of patients among our many other duties. Today only a registered nurse would be allowed to do many of the things I did then!

I was working at the State Hospital when we had a major blackout. It was Thanksgiving and my family was all here at the time to have dinner. The kids were watching TV while waiting for dinner when all of a sudden the screen went blank! My husband blamed the grandkids for fooling around with it. We looked out the window and lights everywhere were out. We listened to the radio and heard that the entire East Coast was in darkness.

My husband made a smart remark about my planning the whole deal with my little friends from Mars. I had recently seen a flying saucer, which of course he didn't believe in. Although I really didn't have to go in to work, I grabbed my uniform, took flashlights, jumped in the car and headed for the hospital to see what I could do to help out with. Upon arrival I was assigned to upper floor, first, second, and third, and found the place in chaos, i.e. Patients crying, supper dishes undone etc.

Then my girls I worked with complained, "We can't wash the dishes as the dish washer won't work with no electricity to run it." I said, "Let's do them the way I do mine at home. We'll just have to wash and dry them without the help of the machine." My patients said, "Carlberg is here so now it's alright and we can go to bed." We got things settled as best we could under the circumstances. When morning came, the electric power came on again and things went back to normal.

I came to love all of my patients, even the most vicious ones. When winter came and the wind howled through the many cracks in the old building I sometimes ran short of extra blankets – but not for long! I robbed the next wards and even took heavy coats from where they were hanging in the closets and they also helped to keep my girls warm.

My years at Northampton State Hospital were mostly happy ones and the people I worked with were super. At bedtime when the patients complained about being shut up in the hospital, I used to tell them, "You have plenty of good food, a roof over your head and no money worries on bills to keep you awake, so calm down, go night, night, and I'll see you tomorrow." My patients were really like family to me.

I remember one time when a priest came to see one of my patients who was very sick. After seeing and talking to her, he came out and told me that she wanted to die but didn't want to hurt me by doing so. He said I should tell her it was okay to die. After he left, I went in and told her that although I would miss her, it was okay for her to die as she was so sick. She died the same day!

My career at the State Hospital ended when I broke my hip while on the job and was retired on disability. I was sixty-two years old.

My Hot Air Balloon Rides

My daughter Rose moved to California and it was there that her daughter Sharron and son Michael grew up. Michael eventually became part owner of a Hot Air Balloon business and was later joined in the business by his son, Michael Junior. I went for a visit to California in my seventies in mid July 1995 where my grandson & great grandson, gave me my first Hot Air Balloon ride. (A "Chase" truck always followed to pick us up after we landed and to pack up the Balloon). We were up a long time and it was very windy. We had trouble finding a place to land but we finally made it. I loved the ride and wanted to do it again!

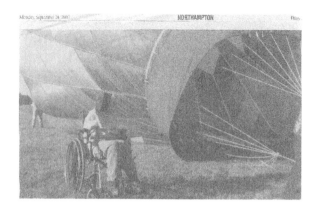

On my 90th birthday, my family gave me another Hot Air Balloon ride, only this time it was in Massachusetts not California! It was a beautiful day and I loved every minute we were in the air. I got my wish to take a second ride in a Hot Air Balloon!

Motorcycle Mamma

As I said when we talked about my late teen years, I have been a motorcycle rider since then but always as a passenger, mostly with a group from Easthampton. In my sixties I decided to apply for a license to drive one, because if you want to get the cobwebs out of your head, if you're upset about something, go for a motorcycle ride, it sweeps it all away.

At the Registry of Motor Vehicles, the person behind the counter asked kiddingly if I though I was the "Little Old Lady from Pasadena" and it angered me so much that I walked out! I had planned to go back the next day, but as luck would have it that was the day I fell at work at the State Hospital and had to retire on disability, so I never got my license.

CHAPTER FIVE: MY GIRLS

Rose, my first cute little dark haired girl, was born on April 18, 1927 during my first marriage to Lloyd Webster as I related earlier in my story. My dad, with whom we lived after my divorce was the only father Rose knew until I married Sailor in 1932 when she was five years old. He was very good to her and treated her as his own daughter for the more than twelve years that she lived with us. But Rose, as she grew up always seemed to be angry and looking for something she never seemed to find. She married an Irish fellow shortly after High School and had two children with him, Sharron and Michael. After a few years she divorced him. She was to marry two more times.

Rose moved to California with her children and third husband Pete and worked there as a waitress and then at Fedco, a large membership store, until she retired.

We stayed in touch, and I visited her there. Also, when she telephoned me once to say she'd been in an automobile accident, I told her that I already knew about it. "How did you get to know about it Ma?" "Well I had a dream last night and in the dream this blonde haired girl got clobbered by a truck. The only problem was I knew your hair was dark." "But it isn't Ma, I dyed it blonde!"

Rose started having physical problems and eventually moved back home to live with me. Her final months were spent at the Northampton Nursing Home where she died at the age of 74 in October 2001.

Sonja, my second daughter, was born on November 28, 1937 – another blonde! She was mommy's girl and would rather stay inside read, and sketch. She had a great natural artistic talent but didn't pursue it. She too married right out of High School like her momma and sister Rose to her first boyfriend. They had six children together.

Her children were lively and one day they called me on the telephone crying. I jumped into my car and rushed to the rescue as they told me their mother had gone crazy and was killing their little friends. When I got there I found out that they had put a line of sugar from the door all around the kitchen table, and there was poor Sonja sweeping ants out the door with a broom!

The marriage lasted twelve years then fell apart. She later married a second time to a man with six children of his own, but the merged family didn't work and the marriage eventually ended in divorce. Sonja went to work for Tapestry Health, a counseling center for women, for twenty years. She recently retired from there.

Judith (Judy), my third and last child was born on February 27, 1940 – another blonde! She was different from both Rose and Sonja. She was a real tomboy who preferred being her father's sidekick, and as close to a boy as he would ever have.

They used to bring our pony, Trooper, right into the house on Christmas where he would get his apple and sugar treats. Judy worked right along side her dad in all the outdoor chores including mucking out the chicken coop and horse stable! At other times she used to amuse herself by finding bird and snake nests (little garden adders).

She went to California right after High School to visit her sister Rose and her family, then ended up staying there for two years. While there, she worked as a bookkeeper in a jewelry store.

When she returned to Northampton, she met and married a young man who was in the service. They had one daughter, Judette, who was born in Tachikawa, Japan where her father was stationed at the time. Once out of the service, they moved to Virginia where her husband was born. They later divorced and Judy and her daughter moved back home to us. She went to work, (supposedly temporarily), at the State Hospital where I was still working. She joined me as a direct care attendant on the wards. She stayed on and eventually became a social work assistant and later went to work for the State at the Springfield Community Department of Mental health as a case manager carrying her own caseload, until she took an early retirement after working for 35 years in the Mental Health System.

I'll be 95 years old in May of 2004 and if it wasn't for Judy's constant care I wouldn't be able to live in my home where I have been for nearly sixty years!

Across the Road From the Railroad Tracks

Across the road from our home on Woodmont Road was a very active railroad track and switching station. For just beyond the tracks when my family was growing up, there was a grain store where Wendy's now stands. There was a tower there and the train engineer had to switch tracks manually. The land from the tracks to the road sloped and my kids, though never going near the tracks, would slide down the hill. When they heard a train coming they'd wave as it went by or slowed up for the grain store or to switch tracks.

Every year the engineer would throw gifts of candy and games out the window for the girls. They would also blow the whistle and always wave at them as they went by. Sometimes when they were stopped I'd bring them some coffee. My kids got so used to the train noise and the house shaking when it passed that when there was a strike for a time, they couldn't sleep! It was too quiet!

In the old days, some people in the area would help themselves to cattle right off the train when it would stop at a nearby railroad yard, and sometimes would drill a hole underneath whiskey barrels on the trains, draining the liquor into jars!

CHAPTER SIX: THE GRANDMA MOSES OF NORTHAMPTON

I've enjoyed many types of "art" work in my long life.

I inherited a love for beautiful garment making from my mother. I've sewed practical clothes for my kids, made them all kinds of costumes, and dressed all kinds of dolls.

I also did some fancy beadwork on pillows for a time.

My greatest love, the one that began when I was twenty but went dormant twice, the major art form in my life–has been oil painting.

I sometimes worked the 11-7 a.m. shift at the hospital and when the wards were quiet and most patients were sleeping, I did a lot of sketching. I always enjoyed drawing and painting. At home I had a few pupils who enjoyed my painting classes and I also taught oil painting at the YMCA. Some of those kids showed real promise.

My "adopted" son, Bernie, tells me that my work is a lot like Grandma Moses, primitive in style with a great eye for color!

I really got back into daily painting when I was 85 and did a painting a day for a long time. I just couldn't paint enough – making up for lost time I guess.

My first painting, which still hangs in my living room, is of Rhododendrons at Look Park. I've given away many of my paintings to family, my neighbors, friends and once to the paperboy. I've also had a lot of exhibits at Hopkins Academy lawn in Hadley, at the Pulaski Park in Northampton, and other places. Many people have bought my paintings so they are now scattered all over the U.S.

A real treat for me (and from their re-actions, for the kids too) was an exhibit of twenty of my paintings at Bridge Street School in 1996 – the same school I attended as a youngster. As a result of this visit there were two articles written about me, one in the local newspaper and the second in the magazine Art Education in the July of 1999 issue. It displayed one of my paintings and a nice write up on me as a folk artist. The part of the article I liked best was "Irene enjoyed her trips to the school and the recognition she received encouraging her to continue to produce art. Students in the school were inspired by "Grandma Carlberg's" presentation, and in response they created art about their memories of the town. This exhibit also inspired a teacher to have her students create art for residents of a local elder care facility."

I continued to do a lot of painting until I was 93 and then slowed up some, but I haven't quit entirely! I like landscapes best. I also do scenes on wooden boxes and paint in acrylic on boards that can be put over the doors. They can be used inside the house or outside as the boards are sealed when the painting is done so the weather doesn't bother them. I think almost anybody can learn to do artwork in one kind or another if they really keep trying!

Why, my paintings even got me a friendship with the Clinton's whom I admire, especially Hillary. My doctor's nurse showed a painting of mine to some friends who sent a copy to Hillary of my I.D., which was in the Gazette. She wrote me a very nice letter complimenting me on my art and encouraging me to continue.

Every time I see that I.D. though, my eyes fall on one question "What was your most irrational act?" and my answer was, "Which one? I ran away from home and family for four days when I was in my early sixties." The rest of that story is that I got as far as a Deerfield Motel where I stayed and promptly called my family after having left a note behind to say I was running away. I kept in touch every day and went back home on the fourth day.

Artists are loving and temperamental!

CHAPTER SEVEN: THE JOURNEY HOME

My father's three girls went to the Catholic Church. My aunt was a cook who worked in a house on the way. My stepsisters would stop there for hot chocolate then go on their way to St. Mary's. I went with them and the priest treated me good – his name was O'Connor too! He blessed my sisters and me too!

I always wanted to be a Catholic but I didn't want to hurt my mother's feelings. She was a Seventh Day Adventist and I had attended some Sunday school there. As I got older and even now I was afraid because I thought my kids would not approve.

I met Father Roy Duquette when I was in the nursing home waiting for the medicine to get out of my system so they could put the pacemaker in. He came around to visit and he was so nice. I just loved him! He had a workman's hands. He had just shoveled snow and when I told him he should let somebody else do it, he replied that it had to be done and so he just did it.

I was baptized as a Baptist so I was received into the Catholic Church through a simple profession of faith in 1996 when I was 88 years old.

I read my new large print Bible every day and say my Rosary.

The Church is my main thing now. I am the happiest I've ever been as I go to Church on Sundays, listen to the word of God, receive my Lord in Holy Communion, and meet some wonderful people. My priest, Fr. Roy is the greatest and Deacon Bernie Fleury and his wife are my very best friends. I never had a son, so in 1999 I "adopted" Bernie and he calls me "mother."

If it wasn't for my good friend June Savino driving me to Church, I would not be able to go, although once in awhile my daughter Judy takes me. (June is my granddaughter Judette's mother-in-law).

It's a privilege to watch my little great grand sons, Casey and Christopher Savino, do their duty as altar boys. They looked so proud when they're carrying the cross or candles.

My journey home to my Father's house took 88 years but I'm finally there!

My life is full. I love my two daughters, my nine grandchildren, and all my great grandchildren too!

It's been a wonderful life and there's more to come!

Swimming Near the Calvin Coolidge Bridge

When my girls, Sonja and Judy, were very young I used to take them swimming at the Connecticut river on the Hadley end of the Calvin Coolidge Bridge near The Sportsman's Club. One day as we crossed the Bridge on the way home and reached the Northampton side, a large milk truck came over the Bridge and plowed into a little old Ford automobile that had stopped on the dry grass causing it to immediately start a fire. I asked a lady who was also walking across the Bridge to watch my girls and after telling Sonja to watch Judy and not let her come across the road. I ran to see if I could help the driver, whose purse I had found in the grass by the car that was now burning, and who was still behind the wheel. I was able pull the lady out.

I screamed for the milk truck driver to help, but he stood in the truck door and didn't move. Guess he must have been in shock. I could hear Sonja and Judy screaming, but I didn't realize why they were screaming and then saw what they were looking at. It was another lady, or what was once a lady. in the back seat or partly under the car. I never saw the other lady and I couldn't help her any way as by then the car was all on fire.

A lady in a house nearby finally called the firemen who took over. They said the lady probably died by breathing so much smoke. I was so upset by this time I took the girls and started walking home and managed to get as far as my friend Mrs. Pelkey's house and fall into a chair. The girls told her what happened and she gave me a full glass of whiskey because she said I was in shock. Then she took the kids and me by the hand to my home, and told my husband what happened.

As for me, I hit the couch and passed out. Pa said a guy from the paper wanted to talk to me but he told him that I was on the couch.

Every time I saw the lady on the street after that she would tell them I saved her life.

Uncle Roy in New Hampshire

Uncle Roy lived up the hill for a mile from our little summer cottage. He took crates of blueberries to market to sell when they were in season. The ladies always wanted a crate to can, so when he was busy he would ask the kids to finish filling the crates. I was one of the kids. So there was one time when as we were working picking blueberries on the other side of the bush it started shaking and someone said UGH! I said UGH back and said you stay on your side and I'll stay on mine. Then I looked around the bush and there was a big bear looking right at me. The kids were yelling, but I didn't feel a bit scared. I didn't know anything about bears. It didn't scare me and Uncle Roy got his blueberries.

Aunt Mary in New Hampshire

Now I'll tell you about Aunt Mary's littlest boy.

You would always find him alone and sitting on the slab of cement that they used instead of a step to get into the kitchen.

Guess what he was doing? Digging up earthworms and eating them! No wonder no one ever wanted to play with him. He always was very quiet and tried to keep his worm hoard hidden, but someone would yell (Ma or Aunt Mary) Tony is doing it again!

I guess it didn't hurt him as he was a banker and well to do when he got older.

Didn't ever look at him no matter what without seeing worms!

I always knew what was happening with my children:

Rose had bought a little house in Los Angeles and a brand new red convertible car. One day she backed it out into the street, a busy thoroughfare, and a truck hit it totaling it and putting her in the hospital with serious injuries.

She called me to tell me about it. When I told her I knew about it she thought her daughter Sherry had called and informed me of the accident, but she hadn't.

I told her, that in my mind, I had seen the accident, knew she was in the hospital, knew all the details, including the fact that she had dyed her hair red.

CHAPTER EIGHT: MY TWO MOTHERS FLORA BEATRICE KING FLEURY AND IRENE MAUDE O'CONNOR CARLBERG

Most persons are delighted if they have one good mother who not only gave them life but also nurtured and loved them through their childhood into adulthood and beyond.

I was one of the lucky men who was blessed with two wonderful mothers, one, Flora Beatrice King Fleury, who gave birth to me and dedicated her life to me, her eldest son, and to my two sisters and brother. My second mother was Irene Maude O'Connor Carlberg, who "adopted" me when she was nearly ninety years old and I was sixty-seven.

<u>My Earliest Memories of Childhood With Mother Flora</u>

I was born on June 14, 1932 while my parents were living in a rental house near the Manhan River. But my earliest memories were of living on the first floor of a two- tenement building where my sister Dolores Mae was born when I was three years old.

When I was four and a half years old we moved to a new house just up the street from our tenement. My dad who was an expert carpenter had built it with some free help from his Carpenter's Union friends. We were now right next-door to my Gram and Gramp King.   Just our two side-by-side driveways separated us.

Mother gave birth to my brother Frank Leon shortly after moving in. She went into labor while cleaning our new floors!

I really gained a second mother as a child because Grandma King attached herself to her firstborn grandson "Sonny" and I to her. My mom had her hands full with me at five years old, Dolores at two years and eleven months and Frank newly born, eighteen months after Dolores, so she welcomed Grandma to help take care of me.

It was from Grandma that I got my first pair of Bantam chickens and she gave me the first flowers for my own garden out back of the garage. I had Iris, Hollyhocks, Yellow Primroses and Sweet Williams. My lifelong love of chickens and gardening started when I was only five or six years old. Gram and Gramp themselves had a big garden and sold peas and raspberries from it and eggs from their flock of chickens.

When I felt sick, I took myself across the driveways to Grandma's house where she would promptly bundle me up in one of her old night gowns and put me in their second bedroom and ask me if there was anything I wanted. I loved chocolates and sarsaparilla soda so, poor Grandpa would be dispatched, regardless of the weather, to march about two miles down town to get Sonny what he wanted. She spoiled me "rotten" as the saying goes.

My mother had been a Methodist prior to marrying my father who was a member of a French Roman Catholic parish. She didn't want a religiously divided home for her children so she agreed to become Catholic, but since she didn't understand or speak French the stipulation was that my dad had to join an English speaking Catholic parish. There was one English speaking Catholic parish in town but it was called the Irish Church. So, my Swiss-French father and English-Indian mother joined the Irish Church and reared their children as Roman Catholics!

Growing Up With My Mother Flora

As I just noted, I raised chickens from an early age and when I got a part-time job on a nearby dairy farm as a teenager I paid for the chicken feed. We sold the extra eggs and I let my mom keep the money for herself – a small token for all she did for me.

47

My menagerie of living things during my teenage years included chickens, rabbits, pigeons, hamsters, goldfish, turkeys and ducks. We also raised a pig or two each year.

I still loved gardening, flowers, small fruits (especially strawberries), and vegetables. Because I either did it myself or assisted my dad with our little farm, my mother made whatever I wanted to eat especially deserts. Angel Food Cake (made from twelve egg whites) was always accompanied by a Sponge Cake (made from the twelve egg yolks) and later the two batters were swirled together to make a "Daffodil" cake. I loved her pies especially apple, strawberry rhubarb, custard and raisin! Her homemade fudge of every kind disappeared in a day or two especially with three kids who all liked it.

All of my 4-H Club members loved it when meetings were at my house because of the refreshments my mother served.

My mom did everything for our family; she even polished all our shoes! I loved her dearly and her mother, Gram King, also.

My dad was a meat and potatoes man, tough roast beef and steak, ham roast pork, fried crisp salt pork, chicken turkey (on holidays), organ meats like liver, beef heart and chicken's feet. He also favored smoked beef tongue, pickled lambs tongues and pig's hocks and pickled eggs!

My dad was a great and supportive father who drove me to all my events too far to walk or bike to. I was in Boy Scouts, 4-H Club and events, Church (Altar Boy), and took tap dancing lessons from the Mooney's in Northampton and in my teens I joined Easthampton Grange.

Dad built all the housing for my animals. He would not allow me to learn any practical carpentry skills, (but I did learn some because I watched him), because he and mom, neither of whom had finished High School, had decided that their first born son was going to college. My dad would yank a hammer out of my hand when I attempted to do some building work. "You're going to school, boy!"

I loved my dad, but as a youngster I was also afraid to cross him because if I did. I got a "backhander" in an instant. This was not a frequent occurrence but I always had a long memory and the few times I got a "backhander" made me leery of telling him anything that might earn me another one.

So, I clung mostly to my mother for emotional support. She was always there with a big hug as was my grandmother. Gram saw my dad whack me once when he caught me and a couple of my friends smoking corn silk in the field across the street from our house, and she told him never to hit me again or she'd call the police. My dad told her to mind her own business, but the feud soon blew over and my dad was back to taking my grandparents wherever they needed to be driven and was very kind to them.

Mom And Dad: Years Of Love, Loss, And New Life

My mom and dad were deeply in love with each other but they had their occasional spats. I remember one particular incident that I'll call – "The Gift of the Magi." My dad kept his loose change in his pocket not in any kind of container. When he put his legs up on his footstool some of the change would spill out and go down beneath the sides of the cushion. I saw mother checking under the cushion and placing the change in a jar she hid in back of a kitchen cupboard. My dad finally began to miss his change. On day, on October first, the day before my dad's birthday he accused my mother of stealing it. My mom got very angry and then disappeared into their bedroom and emerged with a small box that she placed in my father's hands. "Open it," she said. He did and there was a beautiful wristwatch. She turned and swiftly went down cellar with an armload of overalls to put into the set tub to soak. He slowly followed her. After a few minutes, I was nosy so I went downstairs. I found my mother sitting on my father's lap, on an old dusty wooden chair, and they were both crying. My dad kept saying over and over "I love you, I love you, I'm sorry!"

I was seven years old in 1939 when World War II began and nearly thirteen when it ended. Grandma King's health began to decline after 1940. They sold the house next door to us, moved to New York near Gram's relatives for a short while, then moved back to an apartment in downtown Easthampton and finally built a second house two lots down the street from their first one. Gram developed what we then called "Hardening of the Arteries in the Brain," now called "Dementia" and or "Alzheimer's Disease." It took a terrible toll on Gramp. Finally our doctor told my mother that Gram had to be put in the State Hospital to save my Gramp's life. She entered the hospital the middle of April 1946 and six weeks later she was dead. There was a big hole in my heart!

Gramp sold his house and came to live with us. We all wanted him. My mother gained a most appreciative live-in father. She would just mention in conversation at the supper table to my dad that an appliance was in need of repair or possibly replacement and Gramp would go out and buy it for her. He had a good military officer's pension plus some savings and he loved giving gifts.

He helped around the yard, cleaning the chicken coop, gathering eggs, weeding the garden and doing other light yard work. Every once a month on payday, that fell on the last Friday, he'd march up town to cash his military pension check, meet my father after work for a couple of beers and then drove home with my dad for supper. Immediately after the meal, out came Gramp's wallet and he gave each of his grand- children an allowance, the amount varied by age – so I benefited. Five dollars for me, three for Dolores and two for Frank!

My last sibling, Celeste, was born in October 1944. My dad had wanted to join the Sea Bees but my mother would have none of that. So five years after Frank, mother decided that it was time to have her "out of the draft" baby, and I got a little sister! My dad was furious because his buddies were going into the Sea Bees. But since he was doing an important defense job making intricate little wooden boxes used to ship sensitive bombsights in, plus my mother's appeal to the draft board, of which my Uncle Leon, dad's brother, was a member, he was deferred for a year. By the time the year was over in October 1945, the War had ended!

My high school years flew by with 4-H club events, Grange events after I was fourteen, dancing classes and performing in musicals. They were busy but happy years.

Mother During My College And Seminary Years

Gramp King was still living with us when I graduated from St. Michael's High School in 1949 and would stay with us until his death on Christmas Day 1958. Even though I had to give up my bedroom upstairs so Gramp could have a room of his own, and share the larger bedroom with my brother Frank, I never regretted doing so. Gramp was the kindest man who cared deeply for all of us. Although he was a Methodist, he helped his grandchildren learn their Catholic Catechism. He treated my mother as his "little girl" every day and couldn't do enough for her, and my dad and he became best friends!

Ma had plenty of love for all her family and was a great friend to many people. She baked for them, helped clean their houses (those who were elderly) and finally developed a small business selling her baked goods and eggs and doing housecleaning for pay.

I had thought about becoming a priest since the age of ten so during my senior year of High School with my pastor's approval, I applied for admission to St Charles' College in Catonsville, Maryland. I was accepted and began the two-year program leading to an Associate Degree in Classical Languages in 1949.

I was very homesick the first ten months there – five-hundred-miles from home and able to go home at Christmas and then not until June for the summer. Because I couldn't stand to wear starch stiff shirts, my mom bought two aluminum laundry cases. One was always in the mail with my week's laundry in it. Back it would come with the laundry, newspaper clippings and some goodies!

After I graduated from St. Charles I wanted to return to St. Mary's on Paca Street, Baltimore, Maryland to earn my Bachelor's Degree in Philosophy. But my Bishop wanted to send me to Montreal, Canada to the Grand Seminary where I'd have to study Algebra, chemistry, and all my other subjects in French. Though I had taken French courses in high school and college I was not fluent enough in speech or reading to do Academic work other than French, in French.

I vacillated all summer of 1951 and on the day before I was to leave for Montreal I decided I had to finish my Bachelor's degree at our University near my home where I could study in English. Through a friendship with our State Representative, my dad got me accepted and registered in two days and I began my studies as a History Major also seeking teacher certification.

I started dating, continued in the Grange serving as "Master," and with my Gramp's help and the last of my savings I bought a Mustang horse that I named Flicka, so I could ride with my buddy, Dave. My first girlfriend's parents who lived next to us let me use their barn and pasture for free and I worked part-time to support my horse and for spending money. My dad loved to ride and after getting over the fact that I had emptied my account to buy her, rode the horse as much as I did! I had an earned scholarship, lived at home, and had no car of my own, so my college expenses were not great.

But I could not settle down. I wanted to be a teaching priest. I had dated several girls but I felt that I was deserting God by not going on in Seminary. So, in the fall of 1953, after graduating from the University I entered the postulancy of the Holy Cross Fathers at Stonehill College while taking all the philosophy courses required in a single year instead of two because I already had my Bachelor's Degree.

My sister Dolores was now in Nursing School, Frank was in High School and Celeste in Elementary.

I studied hard and earned all A's and a couple of B's at Stonehill, but I was not happy. I missed my social life and my girlfriends. But I had determined to stay until my confessor told me to leave. In March of 1954 we had a long conference. The bottom line was that he told me to go home, get married, and become a teacher! So I did!

I was an emotional wreck. The very trying time of discernment had taken its toll – at five foot nine inches tall I weighed about one hundred twenty five pounds.

At twenty-one years old when I came out, my mother was there to support me. I was so broken that I remember sitting on her lap, hugging her, and crying uncontrollably. She just rocked me as she had when I was a small child. She never gave up on me.

Mother, Marriage, Continuing College, Family, And Career

In April of 1954 I decided to call Lida Healey, the last girl I had been dating prior to reentering the Seminary. We had broken up in the spring of 1953 when I found out that she had a boy friend in the Military Service whom she really cared about and I had been a convenient fill-in while he was gone for months at a time. I had really liked her and on impulse decided to call her because we had been friends for six years in our Grange Youth Group.

The telephone call was very warmly received so I asked her if she'd like to go to a square dance the following Saturday and she said, "Yes." After the dance we went to a burger joint for a snack and had a long conversation. She told me she had discovered that Don had been home on leave at times when she didn't know it and dating other girls so she dropped him. Then she told me how sorry she was for using me and that she had missed me. My "liking" turned to love that very moment and we started dating on a regular basis.

In September of 1954 I proposed marriage and she accepted. I was crazy in love with her and she with me. We set the wedding date for August 20th of 1955 but Hurricane Diane came to our town that week and my fiancée's house was isolated on an island with a huge road washout on both sides of it. One week later on August twenty-seventh, thanks to a hastily constructed footbridge of logs and a rope rail, Lida and her entourage carried their garments over the bridge to her cousin's house where they dressed.

We were so numb from the devastation we had lived through for nine days that I don't remember much about our beautiful ceremony or the reception. We honeymooned at the A Bar A Ranch Resort in the Adirondacks for one week – that week I remember.

I returned on Saturday to my parent's home for supper. My mom loved Lida from the start for they were very much alike – beautiful, spirited women who gave all to those they loved. I had really lucked out in choosing Lida as my wife.

I had to resume my position as Principal, Teacher, and Coach at East Whately Grammar School the following Monday while Lida settled us into our four room apartment less than a mile from her parents. Lida was the one who remained in daily contact with both of her mothers, because my mother looked on her as a third daughter.

I heard about my Mom much of the time through Lida because for the first year of our marriage, in addition to my job, I also was finishing my dissertation for my Master's Degree. Lida, too, went back to work as a secretary at a local insurance office.

I couldn't wait to get home from work after coaching a ball game, but my "romantic French ideas" often got buried in tiredness and Lida spending her time typing my thesis as I wrote it. Nevertheless we were so in love that we made time for each other. Holding her in my arms was the highlight of my day.

When our first anniversary came and went without Lida becoming pregnant, our mothers began to ask, "When are we going to get our first grandchild?" Shortly after our first anniversary those frequent Arabian nights paid off and Lida hugged and kissed me with a special fervor one evening when I returned from work. "Guess what?" she asked? Her look told me the answer. She was indeed pregnant and was to have our first child in April of the next year. We hugged each other alternating between laughing and crying tears of joy. We visited her parents and mine the same night with the news and they too were overjoyed. Both sets of parents would be getting their first grandchild.

In early March 1957, I returned home one evening to find Lida in tears and her mother, frantic! The doctor said she had signs of leaking water from a small premature rupture of the membrane. Though our baby wasn't due for five or six weeks our doctor told her to stay quiet, lay down as much as she could to see if the leakage would stop. It did temporarily and on March thirteenth Lida went into labor and our son was born three weeks prematurely, a small five pounds and five and one half ounces, with flaming red hair, and healthy. Being so small he had to be coaxed to suck and Lida had to feed him every two hours around the clock. She took a leave from work and her mother came to help her during the day so she could catch up on some sleep. I had to sleep in order to work, so my time with him was limited to early evenings for the first several months.

Mother Loses Her Dad, Frank King, Our Hero

In the early summer of 1958, Gramp King began to complain to my mother that he had a sore throat that wouldn't go away. She took him to the nearest Veterans Hospital where he was told he had an infection in his ear. It was infected and he was treated and sent home. He seemed to get better for a short while but his energetic spirit, even at the age of eighty-one, prior to his illness was gone. In late August he returned to the hospital with a sore throat and an earache.

This time, the prognosis was accurate…"I'm sorry Mrs. Fleury, but your dad has esophageal cancer and it has metastasized." My mother, with tears running down her cheeks, asked if there was anything we could do to treat it. We were told we could keep him comfortable with painkillers but we could not heal it. It had spread too far.

"How long has he got to live?" Mom sobbed.

" I can't be exact, but my best estimate is that he will be lucky to make it to the end of this year."

Mother wanted to take him home, but the doctor told her he'd need around-the-clock care (In 1958 there was no available "hospice" like we have in 2008). So, Mom did the next best thing, Gramp went to a nursing home less than two miles from where her home was so all of us could visit him often since we were all living in Easthampton.

The loving Father, Grandfather, and United States Government cited Heroic Soldier began his agony. He lost his voice and had to write notes. The medications given in 1958 had to be given in such large doses to make his pain remotely bearable that he began to live in a half-conscious state. One or another of us visited him every day. Mom was there every day no matter who else came. I went there several nights a week.

Gramp had a roommate, Charlie Smith, who was very kind to him especially during the long nights when as time went on, nothing seemed to stop the pain. He told us that Gramp was a valiant man. Only once did he say that he wished he could kill himself. The rest of the time he suffered in silence or with low moans.

We all wanted to bring him home for Thanksgiving, but by that time he could only swallow liquids and was very weak. As Christmas drew near he was unable to eat or drink.

On Christmas day we all knew the end was very near. He was hemorrhaging but still awake enough to recognize us all with his sky-blue eyes and hand squeeze. We stayed with him into the evening when the doctor told us it looked like he'd go on for a day or two.

We were all at home for an hour or so when the phone rang. It was a little after ten o'clock. We knew what that call was before we answered it.

This was goodnight. It was goodbye. The shrunken hand had moved slowly across the sheet and grasped the crucifix hanging at the side of his bed. Frank closed his tired eyes forever. The victory had been won and he had gone to claim his everlasting reward, the reward of those who are honest and faithful.

Mother's Life From 1958 –1976

Life went on for Flora and her "kids." Dolores finished nursing and married in 1958. Frank apprenticed to our dad after high school and became a fine journeyman carpenter. "Little" Celeste married on our parents' Thirtieth Wedding Anniversary and Flora's nest was finally empty.

She doted on her grandchildren as they came along, loving each of them. Dad and she began to take vacations to Maine and elsewhere and were active in the Franco American Club.

I went back to Graduate School in 1965 and in 1968 earned my Doctorate Degree. My mom and especially my dad told me it was the highpoint of their lives. My dad's "You're going to school boy" had come true. Their oldest son, the first to do so among all my dad's brothers and sister's children, had climbed to the top of the educational ladder.

In 1963, at the age of fifty-five my dad began to lose his balance more and more often, falling once through the cellar stairs hole in a house he, and his brother were building. After numerous tests he was diagnosed with Parkinson's disease and had to go on disability because he could no longer be considered safe on the job. He was one of the first to be placed on Leva Dopa. It worked for a while and he could walk almost completely normally.

Mom loved him dearly and we all sorrowed. She waited on him hand and foot even to cutting his meat on his plate and trying his shoes as the disease progressed. Dad was a proud man – he continued as long as he could to sharpen saws and do small jobs in our house's basement to earn money to supplement his disability benefit. His Carpenter Union friends whom he had served as Secretary/Treasure at the local and county level, saw to it that he had many saws to sharpen and as long as his hands allowed him he continued to build fine pieces of furniture like small tables and desks.

Finally, when Leva Dopa stopped working and he became increasingly physically helpless, he just gave up. One day, mother returned from a hairdressing appointment to find him dead – it was about ten in the morning when she called me and I rushed across town to find my dad with his arms crossed on his chest and stone cold. He was gone from us in this life forever, on August 7, 1976.

My brother and sisters came to see him before the undertaker took him away and ma retired to the kitchen and continued to furiously mix cake batter for a cake. It was her way to cope with grief.

I cried for months. My mom soldiered on – finally having to sell her house and move to an apartment.

She continued to love us all but started a life of her own for the first time since dad's death. She joined Parents Without Partners and became one of their most popular members – everyone wanted Flora to do the cooking for their parties.

She and Lida grew closer. I was in my eighth year as a college professor when my dad died – earning my way through the ranks of assistant and associate professor to full professor that my dad lived to see in 1973.

Ma was proud of all her children and grandchildren, but she always held a special place in my heart as her "Sonny Boy". She kept track of my every move, mostly through Lida, as she was at our house or we at hers for every major holiday, birthdays, baptisms, and other significant family events.

Mother Flora And The Coming Of Age Of A New Generation

In 1980 I went back to "school" to become a member of the first class of Permanent Deacons in our Catholic Diocese of Springfield. Ma was so proud. At my ordination on January 15, 1983, she gave me a beautiful, gold brocade, dalmatic and stole. I treasure it still and I'll be buried wearing it. Mother was present for her son's ordination and first Mass. Early in the morning, six weeks later in February 1983, my sister Dolores in a panic-stricken voice called me. She had found mom unconscious on her bed, couldn't get her on the floor to give her CPR, and called the ambulance.

I rushed to the hospital with Father Jim Cronin to have her anointed. I'll never forget my poor modest mother stretched out stark naked on a surgical table with a cadre of doctors trying to restore her breathing. I objected because mom had told me she did not want to live as a vegetable. I was told that by law they had to try once to restore her breathing. They did restore it but she never regained consciousness. That day I squeezed her hand and she squeezed back – then nothing.

When the doctor told me only the lowest part of her brain, the part that controlled breathing was still functioning – that she was really brain dead, as her executor, I ordered the life support to be ended. She lived on several more days and then went peacefully to the Lord.

As her deacon I did her wake service, assisted and preached at her funeral Mass and did the committal wearing her gift, my golden vestments for the first time.

Even in death Ma was special – she had showed me earlier a list of all her possessions and who was to be given each thing. Anything that could be marked like furniture, she had marked on tape the recipient's name and attached it to it. She left a written note of instructions and asked us not to fight over what she left. She got her wish. We all respected it. She also asked that we meet together at least once a year and this we have done in the twenty-five years since her passing.

After my dad had died, ma had wanted to put a monument on our newly acquired family plot in addition to dad's headstone. I told her to hang on to her small savings. I promised her that when she died I'd make sure that she and dad would have the monument she wanted. So, my wife Lida asked her what she'd like to have for a monument. Ma described it and Lida sketched it.

Over her and dad's grave stands an old rugged cross, carved out of granite, and rising from the top of a huge stone. "Rock of Ages" and "The Old Rugged Cross", were her and Grandma Kings' favorite hymns. She also loved roses and dad loved Lilies of the Valley so I had a single rose with Lilies of the Valley carved into the lower front of the Cross.

I, this lucky man had had his first mother until he was more than fifty years old.

My Second Mother: Irene Carlberg

I was nurtured and loved by my birth mother, Flora, until she died when I was fifty years old.

I remained an "orphan" until the age of sixty-seven when a wonderful lady in her late eighties, who attended Annunciation Church in Florence, Mass where I was serving as the parish Deacon, made an unusual request of me one Sunday after Mass.

I Gain a Second Mother

She and I had gotten to know one another when I greeted her after Mass as she sat in her wheelchair in front of the first pew. As the Sundays multiplied, our greetings became longer conversations.

She was always beautifully dressed with a great taste for colors and I had noticed how attentive she was at Mass. She wept during some of the hymns and at communion time. I was concerned that she was sad about some problems so one Sunday I asked her why she wept.

She answered, "Because I'm so happy to be here. Coming to church is the highlight of my week. I wouldn't miss it for anything!" And she didn't!

At first she could move about with the assistance of a walker, but she needed the wheelchair in church for her back and knees. She lost the ability to walk when she was in her ninety-sixth year

She made an unusual request of me after we had known and talked to each other for more than a year.

"You know, I had three wonderful daughters but no son. I've always wanted a son. Would you be my son?'

I was speechless! She stared intently at me during my silence. I knew that she was far from being senile. Her mind was active and alert. She was very interested and informed in many areas, and a pleasure to talk to.

Irene had a friend, June Savino, who brought her to Mass every Sunday except when her daughter Judy Johnson, who wasn't Catholic, would bring her. June was sitting in the pew in back of Irene, so I whispered in her ear. "Did you hear what Irene asked me?" and she whispered back, "Yes, I did !"

"I don't know what to answer her. How will her daughters and grand daughter (June's son's wife) feel about me becoming her "adopted" son?" June said, "Why don't you ask them?"

So I took Irene's two hands in mine, kissed her on her cheek and replied, "I'd love to Irene but I think I should check with Judy first and she can ask the rest of the family."

I telephoned Judy that week and told her what her mother had asked me to become.

Her reply was almost instantaneous. "We'd be honored for you to become part of our family. Mother is very fond of you and it is true she always wanted a son and never had one. When I asked if she was sure that her two sisters and her own daughter would not resent this new arrangement, she answered, "I'm sure they'll feel the same as I do, and I'd love to have a brother!"

So it was, the next Sunday after Mass, I gave Irene a big hug and said, "You're family welcomes me "mother" so, I'd be honored to become your son and part of your family." She wouldn't let go of me! The tears poured down her face as she said, "I finally have my son!"

From that day in the winter of 1998 until she died ten years later, I had a second mother!

I need to add here that when Irene had first asked me to become her son I wondered how my dear birth mother, Flora, who had been in Heaven for fifteen years, would feel. So I prayed to her for an answer and told her as part of my prayers that I loved her deeply still and would forever. My consenting to becoming Irene's "adopted" son would in no way ever lessen my love for mother Flora. My answer came as I realized how loving a person my mother was, not only to me, and her blood family but to a host of friends besides. I could see her beautiful smiling face and feel her arms hugging me. "It's okay, make Irene happy during her final years. You love each other and love is meant to be given away – to be shared. Our love relationship will never change. Say "yes to her."

From the day I said "yes" to Mother Irene, I was included in all her family celebrations for her birthdays and Mother's Day. I started calling her mother. Ears and eyes picked up at communion time when I brought the cup to her and said before handing it to her, "Mother, the blood of Christ." Gradually the congregation became used to me calling Irene, "mother", and she calling me, "son".

To anyone who asked, "Why do you call her "mother" and she calls you "son", I gave this polite but brief answer: "Irene asked me to become her son and I said 'yes'".

When Mother couldn't make it to Mass because she was ill, had no ride or the weather was bad, I would go to her home. We'd pray together, I'd give her Holy Communion and we'd have a nice visit.

I was told repeatedly, by various members of her family, how much these visits meant to her.

She knew just when I was supposed to come. As I entered the door of her front porch, I'd see her smiling face peeking out between the parted curtains next to her lounge chair. I knew I was wanted.

When the weather was good in the summer, and just before Christmas, June and Judy would bring Mother Irene to our house for lunch that we all enjoyed.

The Life of Mother Carlberg

As I wrote in the introduction to the Wing Walker, America has been blessed with many bold, daring, ahead-of-their-time women. Irene Carlberg was one of those women who lived ninety-one years in the 20th Century and seven years and two months in the 21st Century. When she saw a biplane, she wanted to ride on its wings – a motorcycle, she had to drive it – another plane, she had to fly it. In her nineties she was given a hot air balloon ride and didn't want to come down. She made the front page of the newspaper with a picture of her peering over the edge of the balloon's gondola. A costume maker, a nationally recognized folk artist, a coach to children learning to dance and their taxi driver everywhere – helped mentally ill persons in a large impersonal hospital, serving them in every way she could including advocating for them to her own detriment! But like the rest of the people, especially when we were young, we make mistakes, sometimes nearly fatal ones! Her first short marriage at the early age of seventeen, and its violent end, could have ruined the rest of her life. She defended herself in the best way she could in the legal atmosphere of the early 20th Century wherein women were at a definite disadvantage when it came to divorce and child support. She fought to survive poor decisions on her part, for herself and her child's sake, and she went on to live a creative life of hard work, and loving and giving to her family and many others as well.

In 1932, six years after the end of her first marriage, Irene met a rodeo rider, Irving Carlberg at a rodeo she attended in Northampton, Massachusetts. They fell in love and were married in the fall of that year. Her relationship with "sailor," Pa, Carlberg (he always wore a seaman's cap) would last for forty-eight years until his death in 1980. He adopted Rose, Irene's daughter from her first marriage, and together they had two daughters, Sonja and Judy.

Her girls took dancing lessons so Mother became an expert and creative costume maker for the shows they were in and for others as well. I have two miniature figurines that she made intricate costumes for.

But her real love was for painting in oils. When I saw her work I called her the "Grandma Moses of Northampton." Most of her paintings were in Moses' primitive style especially her "above the doorway" panels, and Shaker boxes. She loved country and sea scenes and had a great sense of color. I treasure them!

Mother had many local and regional exhibits. Many people bought her paintings so they are now scattered all over the United States. She loved to visit children at schools and she was featured in a local newspaper talking to a class about her artwork.

The Wing Walker

If I live long enough (I'm 76), I hope one day to finish writing a book about her life and times.

Her most daring feat, in my opinion, was to stand between the wings of a biplane in flight, so the book will be called "The Wing Walker".

Mother Irene's Journey Home

It was evident in the early summer of 2005 when Mother Irene Carlberg was in her ninety-sixth year, that she was becoming increasingly feeble in body though her mind and spirit remained as sharp and deep as ever.

She told me that she wanted to write the story of her life but couldn't manage it. She began to give me little notes of events in her life, pictures, and newspaper articles about her. I decided to tape record our conversations that I did on three separate occasions. I knew why she was giving me all this information so I finally promised her as soon as I could I would put her story into a written account. I managed to get it written, my wife typed it, and we gave it to her for Christmas in 2005.

Besides being a creative artist, seamstress, and daredevil, as I've noted, she was also deeply religious. I'll let her tell you this part of her story as she recorded it in the summer of 2005.

"My father's three girls went to the Catholic Church. My aunt was a cook who worked in a house on the way. My stepsisters would stop there for hot chocolate then go on their way to St. Mary's. I went with them and the priest treated me good –his name was O'Connor too!

I always wanted to be a Catholic but I didn't want to hurt my mother's feelings. She was a Seventh Day Adventist and I had attended some Sunday school there. As I got older, and

67

even now I was afraid because I thought my kids would not approve.

I met Father Roy Duquette when I was in the nursing home waiting for the medicine to get out of my system so they could put the pacemaker in. He came around to visit and he was so nice. I just loved him! He had a workman's hands. He had just shoveled snow and when I told him he should let somebody else do it, he replied that it had to be done and so he just did it.

I was baptized as a Baptist so I was received into the Catholic Church through a simple profession of faith in 1996 when I was eighty-eight years old. I read my new large print Bible every day and say my Rosary."

Mother must have learned to love the Bible and to make it a part of her life before she entered the Catholic Church. When I first really got to know her in early 1998 she was reading her old Seventh Day Adventist Bible but was having difficulty with the size of the print. So we gave her a new up-to-date large print Bible and she couldn't get enough of it. She read without glasses!

She was also saying her Rosary but was eager to know more about it. We spent several visits talking about it, and because of her love of scripture, her son gave her the booklet many now use that contains a scripture passage for each of the Rosary prayers. Her Bible and her Rosary were her constant companions.

There's more to her spiritual story. Let her speak again for herself in the summer of 2005:

"The Church is my main thing now. I am the happiest I've ever been as I go to Church on Sundays, listen to the word of God, receive my Lord in Holy Communion and meet some wonderful people. My priest, Father Roy, is the greatest and my son, Deacon Bernie Fleury, and his wife are my very best friends. I never had a son, so in 1998 I adopted Bernie and he calls me 'mother'.

It's a privilege to watch my little great grandsons, Casey and Christopher (Savino) boys. Do their duty as altar boys. They looked so proud when they're carrying the cross or candles.

My journey home to my Father's house took eighty-eight years but I'm finally there.

My life is full. I love my two daughters, my nine grandchildren, and all my great grandchildren too!

It's been a wonderful life and there's more to come!"

And there was – nearly three years more!

Reaching The Fullness Of Life: Mother Irene's Last Three Years

There was a lot of loss for Mother Irene which had begun with the death of her oldest daughter Rose in 2003 and personal suffering to match but she kept the same indomitable attitude, looking forward, never complaining, and grateful for anything anyone did for her.

In 2006 her grandson, Donnie, returned as a military veteran to work and to live with his grandmother to help her youngest daughter Judy, care for Mother as she became increasingly unable to do many things without assistance.

One of her greatest sufferings was her inability to be present at the Sunday Liturgy during her last several months. I brought Jesus to her. She received Him devoutly but she and I knew it was not the same for her because she wanted to be present to hear the music, listen to the word of God, pray with her friends, see and hear the Eucharistic Prayer as well as receive Him. But she accepted what she could not change.

On January 10, 2007, Mother lost her second daughter, Sonja, after a long bout with lung cancer. But she soldiered on despite her increasing physical disabilities.

On September 24, 2007 she made the local newspaper's front page when she, went on a hot air balloon ride and loved every minute of it. The front-page picture showed her peering over the edge of the gondola. She didn't want the flight to end. At ninety-eight years and four months   she was still the daredevil woman of her youth. If she really wanted to try something she did!

On November 18, 2007, Mother had a dream in which she was sliding down a hill. She looked back and saw her husband all bathed in light and he was dancing with this beautiful girl. But her husband (while on earth) didn't dance!

So she said to him, " I want you to dance with me." He reached out his hands to me and we danced together. I didn't want it to stop, but he told me I had to go back for now. He'd reach out for me when it was my time.

Mother told me she was at peace now that I had come to her, and that I was to have her wakened whenever I came to visit, as I brought her Holy Communion. She would hug me and hug me as she was so happy, and said "You are my son forever."

We spoke of Heaven and how we'd be together forever – her loved ones – husband – daughters – me. I told her how lucky I was to have had two wonderful mothers and how much she would have loved my birth mother. She and Irene were so much alike – bakers, seamstresses, great mothers, always reaching out to help others, full of life, loving music, dancing and nice clothes, however, one big difference was that Mother

Irene always wore a different colored beret on which she had sewn fancy buttons or pieces of jewelry.

We talked about her wishes for her funeral when the time came., and that she needed to make her wishes known to Judy who was her executor. She told me she wanted me to be in charge of her rites. I told Judy about our discussion and that Mother wanted to talk about it. and it would not depress her.

In early January 2008, her grandson, Donnie, whom she dearly loved and who had been her live-in caregiver, assisting her daughter Judy, died suddenly under tragic circumstances. When I heard the news, I went immediately to her house. She was crying but not for herself! All she could say over and over was, "I hope he didn't suffer!" Before Donnie's death, Mother has lost the ability to stand on her own and had to be lifted in and out of bed, to be toileted or to be taking by wheelchair and lifted into her favorite living room chair where she sat during the day.

Judy continued to fill this arrangement, until she could no longer do it alone and asked her mother's neighbor if he could assist her. Not knowing how to lift someone who was so fragile, and being so strong, unfortunately this caused Mother's sides to bruise, which Judy discovered a few days later while doing her bed care. Mother never complained that it was hurting her, but finally admitted that it did and Judy drove her to the local Emergency Room to have her condition evaluated.

Upon arrival at the E.R., Mother announced in a loud, clear voice for all to hear, that she didn't want anyone to think for one moment that she had been abused. Mother was admitted for a couple of days and was then transferred to a local nursing home for a short rehab. It was there that she developed a serious infection and near the end of January was taken to the Emergency Room at our local hospital. I joined Judy and her daughter Judette after Mother was admitted said she wanted to receive the Sacrament of the Sick and I called a priest friend of Mother's who came, prayed with her, and anointed her.

That day marked the beginning of a steady decline in her strength. She began to eat less and less and her problems increased. Judy spent hours with her each day and Judette stayed around the clock. Her granddaughter Sharron came from California, as soon as she was notified and also spent every day with them. I came every day and stayed as long as I could.

We talked about whatever Mother wanted and could talk about and we prayed together. She could no longer swallow solid food so her final deprivation was Holy Communion.

She became increasingly silent and slept more and more. I saw her alive for the last time on the evening of February 18th. Shortly after 9:00 a.m. the next morning, Judette called me to tell me that Mother had just died and that she wanted to place the phone to Ma's ear, which she did. I prayed aloud the special prayer for someone who had just died – she heard me whether in this life or the next!

For ten days she had been prayed for in her presence and with her response for as long as she could speak. She knew she was loved by her entire blood family and me, her "adopted" son.

Her longing is over. She now lives Jesus final promise "whoever eats this bread and drinks this cup will live forever." She no longer has to see Jesus by faith! She now sees him face to face.

The final paragraph of her funeral homily says it all:

Mother, as we celebrate today your entrance into glory, remember us who remain. Pray for us as we pray for you so that we will persevere in faith, hope, and love as you did, and one day join you in eternal life.

We miss you but we will see you again!

May you be blessed, Mothers Irene and Flora

For all the blessings you have been to others...

Printed in Great Britain
by Amazon

75215015R00047